Lemon-Aid

Tips for home and

A collection of amazing hints and tips for using lemons!

(im)PulsePaperbacks

A Brief History of Lemons

Once known as "the golden apples" or "the golden fruit", and historically used as a valuable trading tool by their countries of growth, lemons are one of the oldest cultivated fruits in our history. There is some contention as to the precise origins of this popular and universally versatile fruit, but it is widely believed that lemon trees were first found in India, dating back some 4,000 years. Early connections to Northern Burma and China are also documented.

Having spread over a number of centuries into Persian and Arab territories, the name lemon comes from the Arabic, (and Persian), word, "limun", and mention of their existence and use was first recorded in Arabic literature in the 10th Century. Their use and popularity widened further afield to the Mediterranean, although the exact chronology of this journey is debated.

During the travels of Italian explorer, Christopher Columbus, he carried lemon seeds from Europe to the island of Hispaniola in 1493; consequently, the subsequent Spanish conquests of the New World served to spread lemon seeds even further. It's also believed that being aware of their medicinal properties; Portuguese sailors would plant lemon seeds during their sea journeys.

Following a large number of deaths amongst British fleets in the 18th Century, Scottish physician, James Lind, pioneered the treatment and prevention of scurvy using vitamin C rich lemons in 1747. Despite the fact that Lind's ideas were not based upon the benefits of vitamin C, the administering of lemon juice to the British Royal Navy proved successful and many lives were saved. Unfamiliar with the fruit, the sailors originally believed lemons to be overripe limes, hence the nickname, "limeys", being given to the sailors because of their medicinal consumption. Of course, they should actually have been nicknamed, "lemonys", instead!

The lemon tree flowers continuously throughout the year, successfully producing fruit for most of its bloom; which incredibly means it can produce between 2,500 and 3,000 fruit in one year alone! Although originally mainly cultivated for its inner fleshy, sour fruit, (or pulp); the lemon rind, (or zest), contains the fruit's perfumes and oils and can be removed and used for flavouring and garnishing.

"When fate hands you a lemon, make lemonade."
Dale Carnegie (1888-1955)

Lemons have been used through the ages for a variety of medicinal purposes and women soon twigged on to the most basic beauty secrets, such as whitening teeth, freshening breath and even reddening their lips!

Predominantly having been utilised for ornamental and medicinal use, it wasn't until the late 18th Century, early 19th Century that lemons began to be used for the cooking and flavouring purposes that we are now familiar with. Today, lemon trees grow in abundance in subtropical climates world-wide, such as; India, Sri Lanka, Mexico, Egypt, California, Florida, the West Indies and the Mediterranean.

This ancient and widely used fruit has an abundance of uses, ranging from culinary and cleaning properties to health and beauty. Read on…

Lemon cleaning!

When we think of the distinctive aroma of lemons we're likely to think of words such as; fresh, sharp, zesty, zingy, crisp, refreshing… all words that we associate with a clean environment. No wonder lemons are popularly used as an 'ingredient' to scent shop-purchased cleaning products. But no matter how lovely some of these products may smell, or how effective they appear to be, we can't escape the fact that they contain undesirable chemicals which pollute our bodies and our environment. They also add unnecessary cost to our shopping budgets!

Getting back to nature with the fresh citrus scent and antiseptic and antibacterial properties of lemons is easy, effective and fabulously economical! Cleaning your home with these powerful and versatile fruits will give you a fresh smelling, sparkling home – and your cleaning prowess will be the envy of all your friends!

Homemade Powerful Kitchen Cleaner

2 tbsp lemon juice
1/2 tsp bicarbonate of soda
1 tsp Borax
2 cups of hot water
1/2 tsp liquid soap

Place all of the ingredients in a mixing jug and mix together until dissolved. Pour into an empty spray bottle and use!

The humble lemon has many versatile uses around the home, particularly in the kitchen. Here are a few ideas to help you be gentler to both the environment and your purse!

Air-Freshener
Freshen up any nasty-niffs in your kitchen by boiling some freshly cut-up lemons in a saucepan for half an hour, (with the lid removed).

Cheese Graters
Remove cheese and other sticky foods from a grater by rubbing the fleshy side of a lemon over the affected area. Rinse with cold water and wash as normal.

Coffee & Tea Stains
Remove coffee and tea stains from the inside of cups by placing a lemon skin in cold water until it becomes inflated, then pouring the water, (with the skin), into the stained cup – leaving it to soak for 3-4 hours. Pour out the liquid and wipe with a clean cloth.

Cooking Cabbage
It might taste good and be healthy, but let's face it – cooking cabbage stinks! To reduce the smell, add half a lemon in the water you're boiling your cabbage in – and don't overcook the cabbage, it makes the smell ten times worse!

Copper Pots
Clean copper pots by rubbing a cut lemon, (pulp side), with salt and scrubbing the pots well. Rinse and buff with a soft cloth to get a brilliant shine.

Freshen-up Your Dishwasher
For foul and musty smelling dishwashers add 55ml, (1/4 cup), of lemon juice in the soap dispenser and run the machine on a wash cycle, whilst empty. Your dishwasher will look and smell lovely, as well as being freshly sanitized.

Lemon Dishwasher Detergent

1 1/2 tsp fresh lemon juice
110ml/1/2 cup of water
110ml/1/2 cup of Castile soap
55ml/1/2 cup of white vinegar
3 drops tea tree extract (or oil)
Baking soda

Mix all of the ingredients together, (expect the baking soda). Pour into a squeezy bottle. Use 1 teaspoon in the first wash cycle and 1 tablespoon in the automatic soap dispenser for a standard size dishwasher. Sprinkle a handful of baking soda over the dirty dishes and in the bottom of the dishwasher, this will absorb odours and boost the detergent's cleaning power.

Fruit Stains
Remove fruit stains, (especially stubborn berry stains!), by rinsing your hands in lemon juice.

Grease
To clean tough grease spots, soak a sponge or cloth in lemon juice and wipe over the greasy area.

Grout
Clean grout around kitchen tiles by applying lemon juice direct to the area and scrub with a toothbrush, or small scrubbing brush.

Kettles
As a preventative measure against limescale build-up in your kettle, place some lemon peel in the bottom of the kettle, fill with water and bring to the boil. Leave the peel in overnight. Remove the peel and rinse out well the following morning for a limescale-free kettle!

Microwaves
Give your microwave a clean, as well as a lovely fresh smell by placing half a lemon in a bowl of water and cooking in the microwave for 5 minutes. Remove the bowl and wipe the insides of the microwave with a cloth to give it a clean.

Microwave Cleaner

6 drops of lemon essential oil
1 tsp vinegar
30g/1/4 cup of baking soda

Combine all of the ingredients to make a paste. Apply to the walls and floor of the microwave with a soft cloth. Leave for 5 minutes, rinse well and leave the microwave door open to air-dry for 20-30 minutes.

Nasty Niffs!
Remove strong or pungent smells from your chopping boards by washing the board with washing-up liquid and water, followed by rubbing the surface with the flesh of a lemon half. Leave for 2-3 hours and rinse off. This will act as an antibacterial agent too!

Rust
Treat rust stains on a stainless steel sink, (or surface), by making a paste of cream of tartar and lemon juice. Wipe the mixture onto the stained areas and buff off gently.

Refrigerators
Give your refrigerator a refreshing smell by wrapping slices of lemon in some gauze and placing it in your refrigerator. Replace them every 2-3 days.

Sinks

Make a cleaning paste for sinks by mixing lemon juice and salt together and applying it to the surface with a sponge cleaner. Rinse well with cold water.

Soap Scum

Get rid of unwanted soap scum and hard water stains by rubbing a halved lemon around your sink. Leave for 5 minutes, then rinse with cold water.

Stains

If you've tough stains on work surfaces, cover with a few drops of lemon juice and leave for 4-5 minutes. Rinse off with cold water and dry. If the stains are deeply ingrained, make a paste out of lemon juice and bicarbonate of soda and apply it to the stained area. Leave for 2 hours and then wipe clean.

Tough Dishes

Remove caked on food from dishes by pouring lemon juice over the offending items and letting them soak for 15 minutes. Rinse off and wash with washing-up liquid, as normal.

Waste Disposal

To freshen up a smelly waste disposal unit, slice up a lemon and put it into the disposal unit. Turn the unit on for a few minutes, with running cold water, until the lemon has gone. The natural chemicals in the peel will kill bad smells and dissolve built up food.

To eliminate waste disposal odours and clean and sharpen blades, grind ice and lemon rinds together until pulverised.

Wiffy Bins!

If your bins are beginning to pong, rinse in a solution of warm water mixed with 1/2 fresh lemon juice and 55ml/1/2 cup of white vinegar.

Wiffy Ovens!

To neutralize lingering smells in your oven, (particularly fish!), place half a fresh lemon on a baking tray and place in the still-warm oven. For your microwave oven, cut up a lemon and place it in a large bowl of cold water in the microwave. Heat on high for 4-5 minutes.

Bathroom cleaning

Homemade Powerful Bathroom Cleaner
2 tbsp lemon juice
1/2 tsp bicarbonate of soda
1 tsp Borax
2 cups of hot water
1/2 tsp liquid soap

Place all of the ingredients in a mixing jug and mix together until dissolved. Pour into an empty spray bottle and use!

Baths
Clean a grubby bath by dipping half of a lemon in baking soda, borax or salt and rub around the bath. Rinse well with cold water and dry with a soft cloth.

Grout
Clean grout around bathroom tiles by applying lemon juice direct to the area and scrub with a toothbrush, or small scrubbing brush.

Hard Water Spots
Remove hard water spots and rust stains, by applying neat lemon juice to the affected area; let stand until the spot disappears.

Limescale
To clean and prevent limescale on shower panels and bathroom tiles, make up a plant mister from the juice of 2 lemons mixed with water. Spray on and wipe after showering.

Shower Doors
Give shower doors an extra sparkle by applying lemon juice with a sponge and then drying them with a crumpled newspaper.

Taps
Spruce up your taps by rubbing lemon skin around them; it'll remove stains and give them a great shine.

Laundry

Brighter than Bright Whites!

For beautiful, bright whites, cut a lemon into slices and place in an appropriately sized wash bowl, followed by boiling water. Leave to cool to between 30C and 40C; depending on the fabric and add the laundry items. Leave to soak for about 1 hour, rinse with cold water and wash, as normal – or; add 110ml, (1/2 cup), of lemon juice to the rinse cycle of your washing machine. Hang the clothes out in direct sunshine for both techniques to enhance the brightening effect.

Everyday Stains

Remove everyday laundry stains by diluting some lemon juice with an equal amount of water and dabbing the stains with the mixture, using a cotton bud, (Q-tip). Rinse with cold water and wash, as normal. Hanging your laundry outside in the sunshine will assist the processes of bleaching further.

Ink Stains

Get rid of annoying ink stains by dabbing lemon juice onto the stain. Leave for 10 minutes then put through a cold wash.

Rust Stains

Remove rust stains from white cotton by adding 225ml, (1 cup), of lemon juice to your washing machine cycle.

Shoes

Buff black or tan leather shoes with lemon juice for a refreshing shoe-shine.

Socks

A tried and tested way of whitening grey or discoloured socks, is to boil them in a pan of water with a couple of slices of lemon. Works like a dream on mucky sports socks!

Stubborn Stains

For removing more stubborn stains, mix some cream of tartar and lemon juice together in a bowl and combine until a paste-like consistency. Apply the paste to the stain and leave for 45-55 minutes, checking regularly to ensure that the paste doesn't bleach the garment too much. Rinse with cold water and wash, as normal.

Trainers & Sports Shoes

Clean and brighten dirty, grey trainers and sports shoes by mixing water and lemon together in a spray bottle, and spraying the offending articles with the mixture. Place them in the sunshine, (preferably), for 45-55 minutes. Rinse with cold water and wash, as normal.

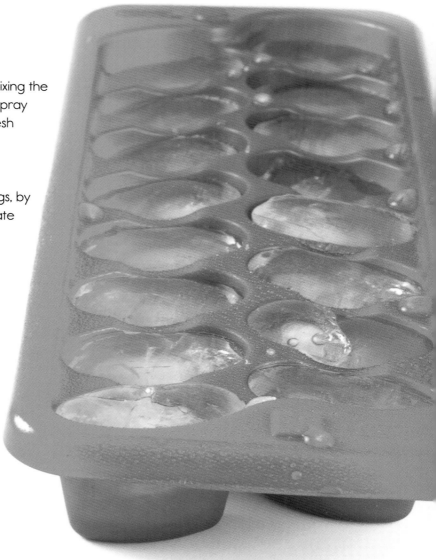

Air-Freshener

Keep a handy air-freshener in your fridge by mixing the juice of a lemon with water and keeping it in a spray bottle. Spray around your house to create a fresh and zingy scent!

Brass

Clean tarnished and dull brass fixtures and fittings, by making a paste from lemon juice and bicarbonate of soda. Mix together well and apply to the appropriate areas. Rub gently, in a buffing motion, until shining.

Brighten Veggies!

Add a squeeze of lemon juice to boiling green beans, broccoli or cauliflower to brighten the colour of the vegetables!

Buttermilk

Ran out of buttermilk? Substitute it for 225ml/1 cup of milk with 1 tablespoon of lemon juice. Works a treat!

Citrus Ice Cubes

Make citrus ice cubes for a refreshing drink accompaniment. Add very thin slivers of lemon skin to the water in your ice cube trays, before freezing.

Copper

Give copper pipes, pans or fixtures a real treat by cutting a lemon in half, dipping it in a bowl of salt and rubbing the copper, using the lemon like a scouring pad. Your copper will come up shining like a new penny!

Culinary

Lemons are a firm friend to any kitchen and its resident cook! Versatile and economical, they're perfect for many culinary uses. And if you want to make your kitchen look and smell fabulous, try arranging some lemons on a large decorative plate or bowl. Looks great!

Diet Desserts

Add a squeeze of fresh lemon juice to diet desserts if you're not keen on their bitter aftertaste. This will also assist in clearing your pallet.

Finger Wash

Add slices of lemon to a bowl of warm water and place at close hand when eating greasy or messy finger food, such as chicken wings or spare ribs.

Firmer Fish

Add lemon juice to your cooking liquid when poaching fish; this will make the fish firmer and whiter to serve.

Food Sanitizer

A great green-cleaner for fruit and meat sanitizer; add the juice of a lemon and water to a spray bottle and store in the refrigerator.

Use to spray salad, fruits and vegetables clean. Spray meat to kill bacteria which could harm – this won't adversely affect the taste of the meat as the bacteria will neutralize the tang of the lemon juice.

Lemon Oil Furniture Polish

10 drops of pure essential lemon oil
2 tablespoons of lemon juice
A few drops of olive oil or jojoba

Mix together well. Dip in a soft cloth
and buff furniture gently.

Furniture Polish

Make a citrus-smelling furniture
polish by combining 1 part lemon
juice to 2 parts olive oil; rub gently
over furniture and buff for a
refreshing shine.

It's thought that the olive oil is good
for preventing new stains on
furniture too! Only make up as
much polish as you need in one go,
to ensure that each batch is fresh.

Guitars

Clean guitars and other string instruments with lemon juice, it cleans as well as adds shine to the surfaces.

NB: Do not use on maple-based guitars.

Hoover Bags

Another way in which to freshen-up your home, is to squeeze a quarter of a lemon into your hoover bag, before vacuuming.

Humidifiers

Eliminate unpleasant odours in your humidifier by pouring 4 teaspoons of lemon juice into the water.

Lemon Zest

Freeze lemon rinds and grate them when zest for recipes is needed.

Mushrooms

When sautéing mushrooms, squeeze in some lemon juice to keep them white and firm.

Marble – Warning!

Do not clean marble surfaces with lemon as this can etch the surfaces.

Metal & China

Lemons are great for cleaning metal and china, just combine some lemon juice with soap and gently rub for a fabulous finish.

Natural Preservative

Preserve food longer and avoid food turning brown when it sits for too long. Sprinkle sliced fruits, such as apples, pears, bananas and pineapple with lemon juice and cover. Squeeze a little lemon juice into guacamole and stir in, this will prevent the avocado from turning brown.

Silver

Give silver a brilliant shine by adding a little lemon juice to a soft cloth and buffing gently.

Health tips and uses

Lemons have an abundance of beneficial health properties, both in the treatment and prevention of troublesome health conditions. Lemons are proven to aid digestion, relieve stomach cramps, boost the immune system, destroy harmful, (and even deadly), bacteria, act as an anti-inflammatory and powerful antiseptic… as well as many other fantastic health advantages.

Alkaline Properties
Although lemons are acidic to taste, they actually have an alkaline effect within the body. This is useful in treating the symptoms of acidosis, as well as providing a more alkaline internal environment to the body, which makes illness less likely.

Constipation
Assist your body's natural 'flow' by drinking 4 tablespoons of lemon juice and 1 tablespoon of honey in 225ml, (1 cup), of water.

Cramps
To alleviate stomach cramps, take 3 teaspoons of dried lemon leaves and steep in 225ml, (1 cup), of boiling water. Leave for 10 minutes and drink. Take twice a day.

Diabetes
Lemon diluted in water can be used to quench an excessive thirst of someone suffering from diabetes.

Emergency Disinfectant
Use diluted lemon juice to disinfect minor wounds in the throat or mouth. Either apply directly to the affected areas or gargle two or three times a day.

Hoarseness

Dilute the juice of 1 lemon in 225ml, (1 cup), of hot water. Leave to cool a little and gargle. Repeat 3 times a day.

Insect Bites

Dab insect bites with a little lemon, this will help the healing process and reduce any swelling.

Insomnia

For relaxation and a good night's sleep, take 3 teaspoons of dried lemon leaves and steep in 225ml, (1 cup), of boiling water. Leave for 10 minutes. Add 1/2 tablespoon of honey and drink just before going to bed at night.

Joint & Nerve Pain

Grate the peel of a lemon, (the outer only, not the white pith), and rub into the affected area. Wrap around with a cotton bandage and leave on for 2 hours. The lemon peel will have an anti-inflammatory effect.

Metabolism Booster

The acidic content of lemons is good for quickening the rate of burning food particles in the stomach, boosting the metabolism.

Natural Diuretic

As a natural diuretic, lemons can provide relief to kidney and bladder disorders.

Nosebleeds

Squeeze a little lemon juice onto a cotton wool ball and dab onto the nasal mucous membrane, inside the nose. The lemon juice will draw the tissues together and stop the bleeding.

Poison Ivy

To soothe the awful itching of poison ivy, apply lemon juice over the affected areas. This will also reduce the poison ivy's rash.

Sore Throat & Hoarseness

Juice 1 lemon and cut the peel into small pieces; mix the two together. Gently heat the mixture in a pan and add a tablespoon of honey. Pour into a mug, cool to drinking temperature and drink. The mixture will soothe your throat which should gradually start to feel better.

Stomach Acid

Drink lemon juice, diluted in water, to reduce hyperacidity in the stomach.

Sunburn

Soothe sunburn by applying lemon juice, diluted in water, to the affected area. The juice will act as an astringent and relieve the pain.

Treat Coughs

Relieve a cough by mixing 4 tablespoons of lemon juice with 1 cup of honey and 1/2 cup of olive oil. Heat the mixture gently in a pan for 5 minutes, then stir vigorously for a further 2 minutes. Take 1 teaspoonful every 2 hours.

Vitamin-Rich

Lemons are vitamin-C rich, which strengthens the immune system and promotes calcium production. They also contain free-radical fighting antioxidants and more potassium than an apple; which is particularly beneficial to the heart.

Not confined to just health benefits, lemons are a fantastic beauty aid too! They're 100% natural, devoid of chemicals and additives which overload our systems and clog up our skin – and they're cheap to boot! How could you possibly not have lemons as part of your everyday beauty routine?

Blackheads
Treat blackheads by rubbing lemon juice over the affected area before going to bed at night. Wash as normal the next morning with tepid water. Repeat every other night until your skin improves.

Blemishes
Reduce skin blemishes by mixing the juice of 1 lemon with a tablespoon of honey. Apply the mixture well to a freshly washed face and then rinse.

Body Sugaring Recipe
1/4 cup of lemon juice
1/4 cup of water
2 cups of sugar
Cotton fabric strips

For totally natural hair removal, mix all of the ingredients together in a saucepan and bring to the boil, (to 250F). Pour the mixture into a jar and microwave for 15-20 seconds.

Powder the area of the body to be waxed, (having tested the temperature of the sugar mixture, ensuring it won't scald), and spread some the mixture in the direction of the hair growth. Cover the area with small strips of the cotton fabric and when cooled slightly, pull the cotton off, against the growth direction.

Cigarette Stains
Remove nasty cigarette stains from fingers by rubbing a wedge of lemon over the stained area. Use regularly until the stains begin to fade.

Dandruff
Rid yourself of annoying dandruff. Apply 1 tablespoon of lemon juice to your hair when washing. Shampoo as normal, then rinse with water. Mix 2 tablespoons of lemon juice with 500ml, (2 cups), of water and rinse again. Dry hair as normal. Repeat this process every other day until the symptoms are relieved.

Deodorant
For an emergency 'I've-run-out-of-deodorant' moment, wet your armpits with lemon extract. This will only last a few hours, but should do the job to give you time to get to the chemist!

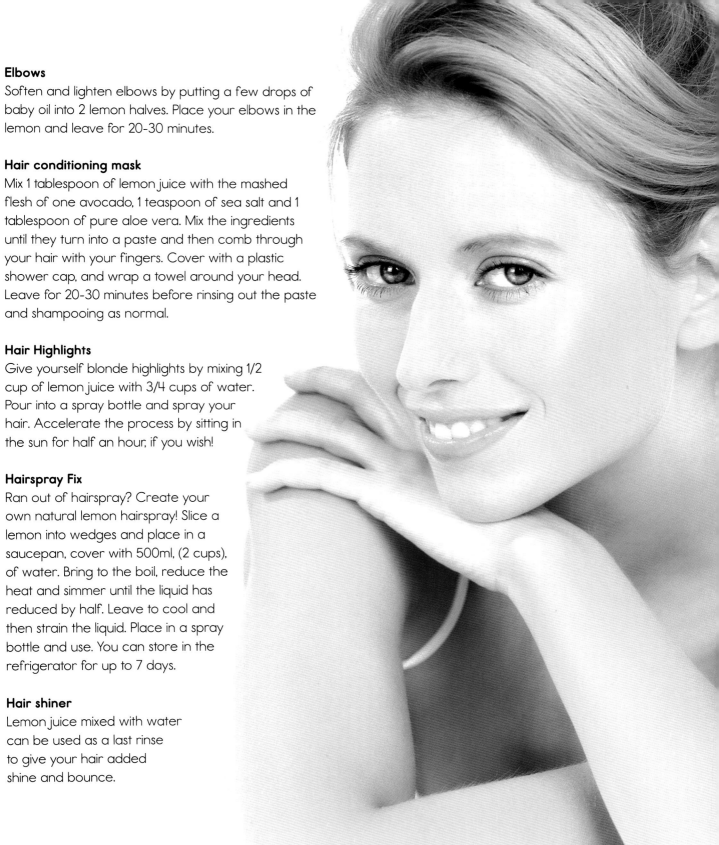

Elbows

Soften and lighten elbows by putting a few drops of baby oil into 2 lemon halves. Place your elbows in the lemon and leave for 20-30 minutes.

Hair conditioning mask

Mix 1 tablespoon of lemon juice with the mashed flesh of one avocado, 1 teaspoon of sea salt and 1 tablespoon of pure aloe vera. Mix the ingredients until they turn into a paste and then comb through your hair with your fingers. Cover with a plastic shower cap, and wrap a towel around your head. Leave for 20-30 minutes before rinsing out the paste and shampooing as normal.

Hair Highlights

Give yourself blonde highlights by mixing 1/2 cup of lemon juice with 3/4 cups of water. Pour into a spray bottle and spray your hair. Accelerate the process by sitting in the sun for half an hour, if you wish!

Hairspray Fix

Ran out of hairspray? Create your own natural lemon hairspray! Slice a lemon into wedges and place in a saucepan, cover with 500ml, (2 cups), of water. Bring to the boil, reduce the heat and simmer until the liquid has reduced by half. Leave to cool and then strain the liquid. Place in a spray bottle and use. You can store in the refrigerator for up to 7 days.

Hair shiner

Lemon juice mixed with water can be used as a last rinse to give your hair added shine and bounce.

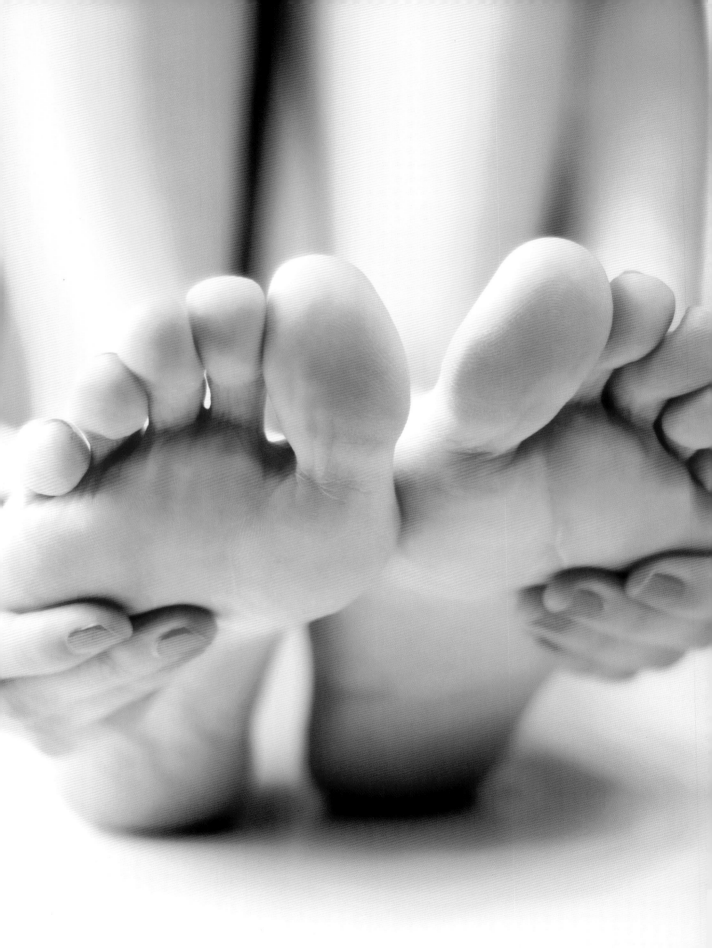

Hand & Feet Skin Brightener/Smoother

Juice of 1 lemon
½ cup of coconut oil
½ cup of sugar
Cotton gloves

Place all of the ingredients in a bowl and mix together well.

Rub the mixture over your hands, or feet, for 1 minute; as though you are giving them a good wash. Use some paper kitchen towel to remove excess sugar from your skin. Put on the gloves and wear overnight. Remove in the morning and wash, as normal.

Handwash

Get rid of garlic, onion or fish odours from your hands by rubbing them with a slice of lemon. Rinse and wash as normal.

Lemon Essential Oil

For many of us, the colour and fragrance of a lemon bring to mind freshness and vitality. While the uses of lemon and lemon juice are countless and varied, perhaps the strongest effect lemon essential oil has to offer is that of lifting our spirits, particularly when we face mental fatigue. Lemon oil helps the body face physical and psychological weariness, most strongly influencing the mind by supporting concentration and the ability to memorize. If you are feeling a little jaded, try this recipe for bath salts.

Uplifting Bath Salts

drops of lemon essential oil
450ml/2 cups Epsom Salts
225ml/1 cup sea salt
Food colouring: 4 drops red, 6 drops yellow
drops of orange essential oil
drops of neroli essential oil
drops of lavender essential oil

In a large bowl mix together the Epsom salts and sea salt first, then add the other ingredients slowly and mix very well. Pour into a warm bath and relax.

Pedicure

Relieve sore and dry feet by applying lemon juice, rinsing and massaging with olive oil.

Spots & Pimples

Clear up spots and pimples by dabbing them with lemon juice, twice a day.

Whiten & Strengthen Fingernails

Whiten and brighten fingernails by soaking fingernails in lemon juice for 5-10 minutes. Mix 1 tablespoon of white vinegar with 1 tablespoon of warm water and brush over the top of the newly soaked nails. Rinse well.

Having been around the house and seen the many uses of lemons, it is time to return to the kitchen for some delicious recipes! And where better to begin than....

Lemon Meringue Pie (Serves 4 – 6)

1 packet of ready-made shortcrust pastry
8 tbsps of lemon curd
6 eggs
300g/10 1/2oz caster sugar

Directions

1. Preheat the oven to 190°C/375°F/gas 5 and grease a 22cm/9in tin. Roll out the pastry to generously fit the tin. Gently lift the pastry into the tin and then spoon the lemon curd on top. Spread evenly to the edges.

2. Whisk the egg whites in a large bowl until they form stiff peaks then whisk in the caster sugar, a spoonful at a time. Spoon the meringue mixture on top of the lemon curd.

3. Bake the pie for about 45 minutes until the meringue is crisp and slightly brown on the peaks.

Lemon Custard (Serves 3-4)

75ml/1/3 cup of double cream
60ml/1/4 cup of milk
Zest of 1/2 lemon (pared)
30g/1/4 cup of caster sugar
1 egg yolk

Directions

1. Place the cream, milk lemon zest into a saucepan and place over a medium heat. Bring to the boil and then immediately remove.

2. Place the egg yolk and sugar in a bowl and beat together. Pour over the boiled milk/cream mixture and mix well. Return to the saucepan and cook over a low heat, stirring continuously, until the custard thickens.

3. Remove from the heat and sieve into a bowl or serving jug. Serve the custard either hot or cold.

Lovely-Lemon Pudding (Serves 3)

225g/1 cup of lemon flesh
1/2 juice of a lemon
1/2 juice of a fresh orange
2 avocados (stoned and mashed)
225g/1 cup of pitted dates
2 tbsps pear juice
2 tbsps maple syrup

Directions

1. Place all the ingredients into a food processor and blend until a thick and smooth consistency. Spoon out into dessert bowls and serve immediately.

Lemon & Herb Pork Chops (Serves 4)

4 pork chops (trimmed of fat)
3 tbsps lemon juice
1 tsp oregano
1 tsp thyme
Black pepper (to season)
1 tbsp olive oil

Directions

1. Place the chops in a glass baking dish and add the lemon juice, oregano, thyme and a sprinkle of black pepper. Make sure that the chops are all covered with the mixture and leave to marinate for 20 minutes.

2. Place the olive oil in a frying pan and heat over a medium heat. Add the chops and cook for approximately 10 minutes, turning once. Cooking times may vary, depending on the thickness of the chops. Serve with a choice of fresh vegetables.

Lemon Cheesecake (Serves 6)

150g/6oz digestive biscuits
75g/3oz butter, melted
225g/8oz cottage cheese
150ml/1/4 pint fresh double cream
50g/2oz caster sugar
Grated rind and juice of 1 lemon

Directions

1. Place the digestives into an airtight plastic bag, tie the bag closed. Use a rolling pin (or a heavy tin if you don't have a rolling pin) to crush the biscuits to form the base.

2. Melt the butter slowly in pan. Transfer the crushed biscuits into the pan, off the heat, and stir well.

3. Spoon the mixture into either individual ramekins, or an 18cm/7in flan case, press down well and chill.

4. In the meantime, push the cottage cheese through a sieve to get rid of the lumps. In a bowl whip the cream until thick.

5. Fold the cottage cheese, caster sugar, lemon rind and lemon juice into the cream.

6. Remove the base from the fridge and spread the topping evenly across the top. Chill for 1 hour before serving with single cream if desired.

Lemon & White Wine Vinaigrette

75ml/1/3 cup of dry white wine
1 tsp honey
55ml/1/4 cup of lemon juice
1/4 tsp salt
1/4 tsp black pepper
170ml/3/4 cup of extra virgin olive oil

Directions

1. Place the lemon juice, honey, salt, pepper and wine in a mixing bowl and whisk together. Gradually add the olive oil, stirring continuously. Cover and refrigerate until ready to use.

Lemon Cake Bars (Makes 32 squares)

Cake base:
230g/2 cups of flour
60g/1/2 cup of sugar
115g/1 cup of quick-cook oats
5 tbsps low-fat butter

Topping:
Zest & juice of 1 lemon
6 tbsps flour
2 eggs
2 egg whites
230g/2 cups of sugar
1/2 tsp baking powder
1/4 tsp salt
Sifted icing sugar (to decorate)

Directions

1. Preheat the oven 180C/350F/Gas mark 4. Lightly spray two 8 inch square baking pans with low-fat cooking spray. Place the oats, sugar and flour in a bowl and mix together. Using a pastry blender, add in the butter and blend together until the mixture reaches a crumble texture.

2. Divide the mixture between the two baking pans and press into the bases of each. Place in the oven for 10 minutes, until the edges turn golden brown.

3. Whilst the bases are baking, place the eggs and egg whites in a bowl and whisk. Add the sugar and beat together until creamy. Add in the baking powder, flour, lemon and salt and whisk until smooth.

4. Remove the cooked bases from the oven and pour the lemon mixture equally over them. Return to the oven and bake for 20-25 minutes. Remove from the oven and leave to cool for 10-15 minutes. Transfer to a wire rack to cool completely. Cut each cake into 16 even squares.

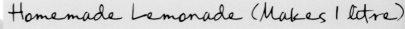

Homemade Lemonade (Makes 1 litre)

4 lemons
100g/3 1/2oz fruit sugar
1 litre sparkling mineral water

Directions

1. Juice the lemons and discard the rest.

2. Add the fruit sugar to the juice, combine with the mineral water and stir well.

Citrus Meringues (Serves 4)

Meringues:

300ml/1 1/3 cups of low-fat natural yoghurt
3 ready-made meringue nests (crushed)
/2 tsp grated lime rind
/2 tsp grated lemon rind
2 tbsps unsweetened orange juice

Sauce:

55g/1/4 cup of kumquats (thinly sliced)
2 tbsps lemon juice
2 tbsps lime juice
2 tbsps water
2 tsps caster sugar
1 tsp cornflour (mixed with 1 tbsp water)
3 tbsps unsweetened orange juice

Directions

Meringues

1. Place the crushed meringues in a large bowl. Add the citrus rinds, orange juice and yoghurt and stir in well. Spoon the mixture into 4 mini-serving bowls, flattening the tops. Place in the freezer for 2 hours, until firm.

Sauce

1. Place the sliced kumquats in a saucepan with the fruit juices and water. Place over a medium/high heat and bring to the boil. Reduce the heat and simmer gently for 4-5 minutes, until the fruit has softened. Add the sugar and stir in the cornflour, stirring continuously whilst cooking. When the mixture has thickened remove from the heat and pour into a small bowl; cover with cling film and leave to cool.

2. When ready to serve the meringues, dip the meringue-filled bowls in hot water for 6-8 seconds, (until they loosen a little), and turn out onto a serving plate. Spoon a little of the sauce over the meringue and decorate the top with a slice of kumquat. Serve immediately.

Grilled Cajun Red Snapper in Lemon & Lime (Serves 4)

550g/ 1 1/4lb red snapper fillets (divided into 4)
2 tsps olive oil
2 tbsps Cajun seasoning
Juice of 1 lime
Juice of 1 lemon

Directions

1. Place the lemon juice, lime juice, olive oil and Cajun seasoning in a bowl, (large enough to take the fillets) and mix together well.

2. Place the red snapper fillets in the bowl and cover well with the dressing. Cover and place in the refrigerator to marinate for 30 minutes.

3. Heat the grill to a medium setting and spray the grill pan with low-fat cooking spray.

4. Lay the fillets on the grill pan and place under the grill for 6-8 minutes, (depending on the thickness of the fillets.) Serve with fresh vegetables and rice.

Sussex Pond Pudding (Serves 4)

350g/12oz suet crust pastry
175g/6oz demerara sugar
110g/4oz unsalted butter, well chilled
15g/1/2oz butter, softened
1 Large Lemon

Directions

1. Grease a 900ml (1 1/2 pint) pudding basin with butter. Roll out the suet crust pastry to a thickness of about 2.5cm (1 inch), and then keep back about a quarter of the pastry for the lid.

2. Line the basin with the pastry. Cut the chilled butter into 8 pieces, then place 4 of these with half of the sugar in the basin.

3. Prick the lemon with a sharp knife or skewer and then press one end into the butter and sugar mixture so that it is standing upright.

4. Press the remaining half of the butter cubes and sugar around the top of the lemon, and then place the pastry lid on top. Trim off any excess from the lid then dampen the edges and pinch all around the pudding basin to seal.

5. Cover with pleated greaseproof paper and foil, then place in a saucepan of boiling water and steam for 3 hours, topping up the water as necessary.

6. Carefully remove from the heat, take off the foil and greaseproof paper and place a plate on top of the pudding. Turn the pudding over, holding the plate in place to invert the pudding. Cut into wedges at the table, so that the 'pond' of sauce runs out.

This traditional recipes allows the lemon to be placed whole in the pudding, but try cutting the lemon into slices and mixing with 1/2 sliced orange and half a dozen kumquats as an alternative.

Lemon Chicken with Parsley (Serves 8)

8 chicken breasts (skinless)
Juice of 2 lemons
110g/1/2 cup of fresh parsley (chopped)
Black pepper (to season)

Directions

1. Preheat the oven to 230C/450F/Gas mark 8. Spray a baking tray with low-fat cooking spray (you may need two trays) and lay on the chicken breasts.

2. Drizzle the lemon juice over the chicken and sprinkle with the fresh parsley. Season with black pepper, according to taste. Place in the oven and cook for 20 minutes. Serve with fresh vegetables or a light salad.

The recipes contained in this book are passed on in good faith but the publisher cannot be held responsible for any adverse results. Please be aware that certain recipes may contain nuts. The recipes use both metric and imperial measurements, and the reader should not mix metric and imperial measurements. Spoon measurements are level, teaspoons are assumed to be 5ml, tablespoons 15ml. For other measurements, see chart below. Times given are for guidance only, as preparation techniques may vary and can lead to different cooking times.

Spoons to millilitres

1/2 teaspoon	2.5 ml	1 Tablespoon	15 ml
1 teaspoon	5 ml	2 Tablespoons	30 ml
1-1 1/2 teaspoons	7.5 ml	3 Tablespoons	45 ml
2 teaspoons	10 ml	4 Tablespoons	60 ml

Grams to ounces

10g	0.25oz	225g	8oz
15g	0.38oz	250g	9oz
25g	1oz	275g	10oz
50g	2oz	300g	11oz
75g	3oz	350g	12oz
110g	4oz	375g	13oz
150g	5oz	400g	14oz
175g	6oz	425g	15oz
200g	7oz	450g	16oz

Metric to cups

Description		
Flour etc	115g	1 cup
Clear honey etc	350g	1 cup
Liquids etc	225ml	1 cup

Liquid measures

5fl oz	1/4 pint	150 ml
7.5fl oz		215 ml
10fl oz	1/2 pint	275 ml
15fl oz		425 ml
20fl oz	1 pint	570 ml
35fl oz		1 litre

This edition first published in 2009 by ImPulse Paperbacks, an imprint of Iron Press Ltd. © Iron Press Ltd 2009 Printed in China